My Favorite

CUISINART
ICE CREAM MAKER

Recipe Book

Sarah Aubert

Contents

Introduction

When I was a kid, summer meant homemade ice cream. My siblings and I would get super excited when we saw Dad pulling out the old ice cream maker from the attic. This wasn't the easy kind—it needed lots of ice and rock salt. It was loud, messy, and took forever, but we loved it.

We'd take turns cranking the handle, always peeking inside to see if it was turning into ice cream yet. The process felt like it took ages, but the reward was amazing. Every spoonful of that homemade ice cream tasted so good because it was made with love and effort. Those summer afternoons, filled with the noise and fun of making ice cream, are some of my best memories.

Today, making ice cream is so much easier with the Cuisinart ice cream maker. No more hard work with ice and rock salt. The Cuisinart is quick, clean, and makes delicious ice cream every time. It helps us recreate those wonderful flavors and try new ones without all the hassle.

This book is a tribute to those old times and a celebration of the new. Inside, you'll find recipes that remind us of the ice cream we loved as kids, plus some new, exciting flavors to try. Whether you want a classic taste or something different, this book has it all.

So, get your Cuisinart ice cream maker ready and start making new memories with your family. Let's enjoy the simple pleasure of homemade ice cream—easier now, but just as magical as ever.

Why Homemade Ice Cream?

Homemade ice cream brings a special kind of joy that store-bought varieties just can't match. Here are a few reasons why making ice cream at home is such a beloved activity:

1. Unmatched Freshness and Flavor

When you make ice cream at home, you get to enjoy it at its freshest. The flavors are more vibrant, and the texture is creamier because you control the ingredients and the process. Freshly churned ice cream, with its rich taste and smooth consistency, offers a delightful experience that mass-produced ice creams often lack.

2. Quality Ingredients

One of the best parts of making ice cream at home is knowing exactly what goes into it. You can choose high-quality, natural ingredients, avoiding the artificial additives and preservatives found in many commercial ice creams. This means healthier and more delicious treats for you and your loved ones.

3. Customization

Homemade ice cream allows for endless customization. Whether you prefer classic flavors like vanilla and chocolate or adventurous combinations like lavender-honey or avocado-lime, you can tailor every batch to your taste. You can also adjust the sweetness, richness, and even create dairy-free or low-sugar versions.

4. Fun and Creativity

Making ice cream is a fun and creative activity for people of all ages. From choosing flavors and mix-ins to experimenting with new recipes, the process is engaging and rewarding. It's a great way to spend time with family and friends, creating not just delicious desserts, but also lasting memories.

5. Nostalgia and Tradition

For many, making homemade ice cream is a cherished tradition that brings back fond memories of childhood. The process of churning ice cream, whether by hand or with an electric maker, often evokes a sense of nostalgia and connection to simpler times.

6. Learning and Experimentation

Homemade ice cream offers a wonderful opportunity to learn about the science of food. Understanding how ingredients like milk, cream, sugar, and eggs interact can be fascinating.

Plus, experimenting with different techniques and flavors can lead to delicious discoveries and a deeper appreciation for the craft.

7. Satisfaction and Achievement

There's a unique sense of accomplishment that comes with making something from scratch. When you take that first bite of your homemade ice cream, knowing you created it yourself, the satisfaction is immense. It's a tangible reward for your effort and creativity.

8. Perfect for Special Diets

Homemade ice cream is perfect for those with dietary restrictions. You can easily make dairy-free, sugar-free, or allergy-friendly versions to suit your needs. This ensures everyone can enjoy a delicious frozen treat, no matter their dietary preferences or requirements.

Primary Methods for Making Ice Cream

Custard-based (French-style) and Philadelphia-style (American-style) ice creams are two primary methods for making ice cream, each offering distinct characteristics and preparation processes.

Custard-based ice cream uses egg yolks, which create a rich, creamy texture and a velvety mouthfeel. The egg yolks are cooked with cream and sugar to form a custard, which is then chilled and churned. This method results in a dense, luxurious ice cream with a deep flavor profile, perfect for those who enjoy a more decadent dessert.

Philadelphia-style ice cream, on the other hand, is made without eggs. It consists of just cream, milk, sugar, and flavorings, making it quicker and simpler to prepare. This style is lighter and often has a cleaner, more straightforward flavor. It's ideal for showcasing fresh, delicate ingredients.

Despite these differences, the end result of both styles is remarkably similar: a delicious, creamy ice cream. The choice between custard-based and Philadelphia-style often comes down to personal preference and the desired flavor profile.

In this recipe book, both styles are included to provide variety and cater to different tastes and occasions. Some recipes benefit from the richness of a custard base, while others shine with the simplicity of a Philadelphia-style base. This way, you can explore the best of both worlds and find the perfect ice cream for any craving.

1. Ice Cream Recipes

Classic Vanilla Ice Cream

Servings: 6-8

Ingredients

2 cups heavy cream

1 cup whole milk

3/4 cup sugar

1 tablespoon vanilla extract

5 egg yolks

Instructions

In a medium saucepan, heat the milk and cream until it begins to simmer. Do not boil.

In a bowl, whisk the egg yolks and sugar until pale and thick.

Slowly pour the hot milk mixture into the eggs, whisking constantly.

Return the mixture to the saucepan and cook over low heat, stirring constantly, until it thickens enough to coat the back of a spoon.

Remove from heat and stir in vanilla extract.

Cool the mixture completely in the refrigerator (at least 4 hours).

Pour the chilled mixture into the Cuisinart ice cream maker and churn for 20-25 minutes.

Transfer to an airtight container and freeze for at least 2 hours before serving.

Chocolate Ice Cream

Servings: 6-8

Ingredients

2 cups heavy cream

1 cup whole milk

3/4 cup sugar

1 cup cocoa powder

5 egg yolks

1 teaspoon vanilla extract

Instructions

In a saucepan, heat the milk, cream, and cocoa powder, stirring until smooth and hot. Do not boil.

Whisk the egg yolks and sugar until thick and pale.

Gradually add the hot chocolate mixture to the eggs, whisking constantly.

Return to the saucepan and cook over low heat, stirring until thickened.

Remove from heat and add vanilla extract.

Cool completely in the refrigerator.

Churn in the Cuisinart ice cream maker for 20-25 minutes.

Freeze in an airtight container for at least 2 hours.

Strawberry Ice Cream

Servings: 6-8

Ingredients

2 cups heavy cream

1 cup whole milk

3/4 cup sugar

1 tablespoon vanilla extract

5 egg yolks

2 cups fresh strawberries, pureed

Instructions

Heat the cream and milk in a saucepan until hot. Do not boil.

Whisk the egg yolks and sugar until thick.

Slowly mix the hot milk into the yolks, then return to the saucepan and cook until thickened.

Stir in the vanilla extract and pureed strawberries.

Chill the mixture in the refrigerator.

Churn in the ice cream maker for 20-25 minutes.

Freeze in an airtight container for at least 2 hours.

Coffee Ice Cream

Servings: 6-8

Ingredients

2 cups heavy cream

1 cup whole milk

3/4 cup sugar

5 egg yolks

2 tablespoons instant coffee granules

1 tablespoon vanilla extract

Instructions

Heat the milk, cream, and coffee granules until hot. Do not boil.

Whisk the egg yolks and sugar until thick.

Gradually add the hot mixture to the eggs, whisking constantly.

Return to the saucepan and cook until thickened.

Stir in the vanilla extract.

Chill in the refrigerator.

Churn in the ice cream maker for 20-25 minutes.

Freeze for at least 2 hours.

Mint Chocolate Chip Ice Cream

Servings: 6-8

Ingredients

2 cups heavy cream

1 cup whole milk

3/4 cup sugar

5 egg yolks

1 tablespoon peppermint extract

1 cup mini chocolate chips

Instructions

Heat the milk and cream until hot. Do not boil.

Whisk the egg yolks and sugar until thick.

Slowly add the hot mixture to the eggs, then return to the saucepan and cook until thickened.

Stir in the peppermint extract.

Chill the mixture in the refrigerator.

Churn in the ice cream maker for 20-25 minutes, adding the chocolate chips in the last 5 minutes.

Freeze for at least 2 hours.

Vegan Chocolate Ice Cream

Servings: 6-8

Ingredients

2 cups coconut milk

1 cup almond milk

3/4 cup sugar

1 cup cocoa powder

1 tablespoon vanilla extract

Instructions

Whisk together all the ingredients in a bowl until smooth.

Chill the mixture. Churn in the ice cream maker for 20-25 minutes.

Freeze for at least 2 hours.

Coconut Ice Cream

Servings: 6-8

Ingredients

2 cups coconut milk

1 cup heavy cream

3/4 cup sugar

1 tablespoon vanilla extract

Instructions

Whisk together all the ingredients in a bowl. Chill the mixture.

Churn in the ice cream maker for 20-25 minutes.

Freeze for at least 2 hours.

Pistachio Ice Cream

Servings: 6-8

Ingredients

2 cups heavy cream

1 cup whole milk

3/4 cup sugar

5 egg yolks

1 teaspoon almond extract

1 cup chopped pistachios

Instructions

Heat milk and cream until hot. Do not boil. Whisk egg yolks and sugar until thick.

Slowly add hot milk to yolks, then cook until thickened. Stir in almond extract and pistachios. Chill the mixture.

Churn in the ice cream maker for 20-25 minutes. Freeze for at least 2 hours.

Cookies and Cream Ice Cream

Servings: 6-8

Ingredients

2 cups heavy cream

1 cup whole milk

3/4 cup sugar

1 tablespoon vanilla extract

20 crushed Oreo cookies

Instructions

Whisk together cream, milk, sugar, and vanilla until sugar dissolves. Chill the mixture.

Churn in the ice cream maker for 20-25 minutes, adding Oreos in the last 5 minutes.

Freeze for at least 2 hours.

Raspberry Ripple Ice Cream

Servings: 6-8

Ingredients

2 cups heavy cream

1 cup whole milk

3/4 cup sugar

5 egg yolks

1 tablespoon vanilla extract

1 cup raspberry puree

Instructions

Heat milk and cream until hot. Do not boil.

Whisk egg yolks and sugar until thick.

Gradually add hot milk to yolks, then cook until thickened.

Stir in vanilla extract and chill.

Churn in the ice cream maker for 20-25 minutes.

Swirl in raspberry puree before freezing for at least 2 hours.

Peanut Butter Ice Cream

Servings: 6-8

Ingredients

2 cups heavy cream

1 cup whole milk

3/4 cup sugar

1 cup peanut butter

1 teaspoon vanilla extract

Instructions

Whisk together all ingredients until smooth.

Chill the mixture.

Churn in the ice cream maker for 20-25 minutes. Freeze for at least 2 hours.

Banana Ice Cream

Servings: 6-8

Ingredients

2 cups heavy cream

1 cup whole milk

3/4 cup sugar

1 tablespoon vanilla extract

2 ripe bananas, mashed

Instructions

Whisk together all ingredients until smooth. Chill the mixture.

Churn in the ice cream maker for 20-25 minutes. Freeze for at least 2 hours.

Blueberry Cheesecake Ice Cream

Servings: 6-8

Ingredients

2 cups heavy cream

1 cup whole milk

3/4 cup sugar

8 oz cream cheese, softened

1 cup blueberry puree

Instructions

Blend cream cheese with sugar until smooth. Mix in milk, cream, and blueberry puree.

Chill the mixture. Churn in the ice cream maker for 20-25 minutes.

Freeze for at least 2 hours.

Salted Caramel Ice Cream

Servings: 6-8

Ingredients

2 cups heavy cream

1 cup whole milk

3/4 cup sugar

1/2 cup caramel sauce

1 teaspoon sea salt

Instructions

Whisk together all ingredients until smooth. Chill the mixture.

Churn in the ice cream maker for 20-25 minutes.

Freeze for at least 2 hours.

Butterscotch Ice Cream

Servings: 6-8

Ingredients

2 cups heavy cream

1 cup whole milk

3/4 cup brown sugar

5 egg yolks

1 teaspoon vanilla extract

2 tablespoons butter

Instructions

In a saucepan, melt butter and brown sugar, stirring until smooth.

Add the cream and milk, heating until hot but not boiling.

Whisk the egg yolks until thick, then slowly add the hot mixture to the yolks, whisking constantly.

Return to the saucepan and cook until thickened.

Stir in vanilla extract and chill the mixture.

Churn in the ice cream maker for 20-25 minutes.

Freeze for at least 2 hours.

Black Sesame Ice Cream

Servings: 6-8

Ingredients

2 cups heavy cream

1 cup whole milk

3/4 cup sugar

5 egg yolks

3 tablespoons black sesame paste

Instructions

Heat the milk and cream until hot. Whisk egg yolks and sugar until thick.

Gradually add hot milk to yolks, then cook until thickened. Stir in black sesame paste.

Chill the mixture. Churn in the ice cream maker for 20-25 minutes.

Freeze for at least 2 hours.

Avocado Ice Cream

Servings: 6-8

Ingredients

2 ripe avocados, peeled and pitted

1 cup heavy cream

1 cup whole milk

3/4 cup sugar

1 tablespoon lime juice

Instructions

Blend avocados, milk, cream, sugar, and lime juice until smooth. Chill the mixture.

Churn in the ice cream maker for 20-25 minutes. Freeze for at least 2 hours.

Cinnamon Ice Cream

Servings: 6-8

Ingredients

2 cups heavy cream

1 cup whole milk

3/4 cup sugar

5 egg yolks

1 tablespoon ground cinnamon

1 teaspoon vanilla extract

Instructions

Heat the milk and cream until hot. Whisk egg yolks and sugar until thick.

Gradually add hot milk to yolks, then cook until thickened. Stir in cinnamon and vanilla extract.

Chill the mixture. Churn in the ice cream maker for 20-25 minutes.

Freeze for at least 2 hours.

Ginger Ice Cream

Servings: 6-8

Ingredients

2 cups heavy cream

1 cup whole milk

3/4 cup sugar

5 egg yolks

2 tablespoons fresh ginger, grated

1 teaspoon vanilla extract

Instructions

Heat the milk, cream, and ginger until hot.

Whisk egg yolks and sugar until thick.

Gradually add hot milk to yolks, then cook until thickened.

Stir in vanilla extract.

Chill the mixture.

Churn in the ice cream maker for 20-25 minutes.

Freeze for at least 2 hours.

Maple Walnut Ice Cream

Servings: 6-8

Ingredients

2 cups heavy cream

1 cup whole milk

3/4 cup pure maple syrup

1 cup walnuts, chopped

Instructions

Whisk together cream, milk, and maple syrup until well combined. Chill the mixture.

Churn in the ice cream maker for 20-25 minutes, adding walnuts in the last 5 minutes.

Freeze for at least 2 hours.

Honey Almond Ice Cream

Servings: 6-8

Ingredients

2 cups heavy cream

1 cup whole milk

3/4 cup honey

1 teaspoon almond extract

1 cup sliced almonds, toasted

Instructions

Heat the milk, cream, and honey until hot. Do not boil. Chill the mixture. Stir in almond extract.

Churn in the ice cream maker for 20-25 minutes, adding toasted almonds in the last 5 minutes.

Freeze for at least 2 hours.

Lemon Basil Ice Cream

<u>Servings:</u> 6-8

<u>Ingredients</u>

2 cups heavy cream

1 cup whole milk

3/4 cup sugar

1/2 cup fresh basil leaves, chopped

1 tablespoon lemon zest

1/4 cup fresh lemon juice

<u>Instructions</u>

Heat milk, cream, sugar, basil, and lemon zest until hot. Do not boil.

Remove from heat and let steep for 20 minutes, then strain.

Stir in lemon juice and chill the mixture.

Churn in the ice cream maker for 20-25 minutes.

Freeze for at least 2 hours.

Brownie Chunk Ice Cream

Servings: 6-8

Ingredients

2 cups heavy cream

1 cup whole milk

3/4 cup sugar

1 tablespoon vanilla extract

2 cups brownie chunks

Instructions

Whisk together cream, milk, sugar, and vanilla until the sugar dissolves.

Chill the mixture.

Churn in the ice cream maker for 20-25 minutes, adding brownie chunks in the last 5 minutes.

Freeze for at least 2 hours.

Caramel Swirl Ice Cream

Servings: 6-8

Ingredients

2 cups heavy cream

1 cup whole milk

3/4 cup sugar

1 tablespoon vanilla extract

1/2 cup caramel sauce

Instructions

Whisk together cream, milk, sugar, and vanilla until the sugar dissolves.

Chill the mixture. Churn in the ice cream maker for 20-25 minutes.

Gently swirl in caramel sauce before freezing for at least 2 hours.

Peanut Butter Chocolate Chip Ice Cream

Servings: 6-8

Ingredients

2 cups heavy cream

1 cup whole milk

3/4 cup sugar

1 cup peanut butter

1 teaspoon vanilla extract

1 cup mini chocolate chips

Instructions

Whisk together cream, milk, sugar, peanut butter, and vanilla until smooth.

Chill the mixture.

Churn in the ice cream maker for 20-25 minutes, adding chocolate chips in the last 5 minutes.

Freeze for at least 2 hours.

Mocha Ice Cream

Servings: 6-8

Ingredients

2 cups heavy cream

1 cup whole milk

3/4 cup sugar

2 tablespoons instant coffee granules

1/2 cup chocolate syrup

1 teaspoon vanilla extract

Instructions

Heat milk, cream, and coffee granules until hot. Do not boil.

Whisk together sugar, chocolate syrup, and vanilla extract.

Chill the mixture.

Churn in the ice cream maker for 20-25 minutes.

Freeze for at least 2 hours.

2. Frozen Yogurt Recipes

Vanilla Frozen Yogurt

Servings: 6-8

Ingredients

4 cups plain Greek yogurt

3/4 cup sugar

1 tablespoon vanilla extract

Instructions

In a medium bowl, whisk together the yogurt, sugar, and vanilla extract until the sugar is dissolved.

Chill the mixture in the refrigerator for at least 2 hours.

Pour the chilled mixture into the Cuisinart ice cream maker and churn for 20-25 minutes.

Transfer to an airtight container and freeze for at least 2 hours before serving.

Strawberry Frozen Yogurt

Servings: 6-8

Ingredients

4 cups plain Greek yogurt

2 cups strawberries, hulled and sliced

3/4 cup sugar

1 tablespoon lemon juice

Instructions

Puree the strawberries and sugar in a blender until smooth. Mix the strawberry puree with yogurt and lemon juice. Chill the mixture in the refrigerator for at least 2 hours.

Pour the chilled mixture into the Cuisinart ice cream maker and churn for 20-25 minutes.

Transfer to an airtight container and freeze for at least 2 hours before serving.

Chocolate Frozen Yogurt

Servings: 6-8

Ingredients

4 cups plain Greek yogurt

3/4 cup sugar

1 cup cocoa powder

1 teaspoon vanilla extract

Instructions

Whisk together the yogurt, sugar, cocoa powder, and vanilla extract until smooth.

Chill the mixture in the refrigerator for at least 2 hours.

Pour the chilled mixture into the Cuisinart ice cream maker and churn for 20-25 minutes.

Transfer to an airtight container and freeze for at least 2 hours before serving.

Lemon Frozen Yogurt

Servings: 6-8

Ingredients

4 cups plain Greek yogurt

1 cup sugar

1/2 cup fresh lemon juice

1 tablespoon lemon zest

Instructions

Whisk together the yogurt, sugar, lemon juice, and lemon zest until the sugar is dissolved.

Chill the mixture in the refrigerator for at least 2 hours.

Pour the chilled mixture into the Cuisinart ice cream maker and churn for 20-25 minutes.

Transfer to an airtight container and freeze for at least 2 hours before serving.

Peach Frozen Yogurt

Servings: 6-8

Ingredients

4 cups plain Greek yogurt

2 cups peach puree

3/4 cup sugar

1 tablespoon lemon juice

Instructions

Blend the peach puree and sugar until the sugar is dissolved. Mix the peach mixture with yogurt and lemon juice. Chill the mixture in the refrigerator for at least 2 hours.

Pour the chilled mixture into the Cuisinart ice cream maker and churn for 20-25 minutes.

Transfer to an airtight container and freeze for at least 2 hours before serving.

Raspberry Frozen Yogurt

Servings: 6-8

Ingredients

4 cups plain Greek yogurt

2 cups raspberries

3/4 cup sugar

1 tablespoon lemon juice

Instructions

Puree the raspberries and sugar in a blender until smooth. Mix the raspberry puree with yogurt and lemon juice. Chill the mixture in the refrigerator for at least 2 hours.

Pour the chilled mixture into the Cuisinart ice cream maker and churn for 20-25 minutes.

Transfer to an airtight container and freeze for at least 2 hours before serving.

Banana Frozen Yogurt

Servings: 6-8

Ingredients

4 cups plain Greek yogurt

2 ripe bananas, mashed

3/4 cup sugar

1 tablespoon lemon juice

Instructions

Blend the mashed bananas and sugar until the sugar is dissolved.

Mix the banana mixture with yogurt and lemon juice.

Chill the mixture in the refrigerator for at least 2 hours.

Pour the chilled mixture into the Cuisinart ice cream maker and churn for 20-25 minutes.

Transfer to an airtight container and freeze for at least 2 hours before serving.

Pineapple Frozen Yogurt

Servings: 6-8

Ingredients

4 cups plain Greek yogurt

2 cups crushed pineapple, drained

3/4 cup sugar

Instructions

Blend the crushed pineapple and sugar until the sugar is dissolved.

Mix the pineapple mixture with yogurt.

Chill the mixture in the refrigerator for at least 2 hours.

Pour the chilled mixture into the Cuisinart ice cream maker and churn for 20-25 minutes.

Transfer to an airtight container and freeze for at least 2 hours before serving.

Blueberry Frozen Yogurt

Servings: 6-8

Ingredients

4 cups plain Greek yogurt

2 cups blueberries

3/4 cup sugar

1 tablespoon lemon juice

Instructions

Puree the blueberries and sugar in a blender until smooth. Mix the blueberry puree with yogurt and lemon juice. Chill the mixture in the refrigerator for at least 2 hours.

Pour the chilled mixture into the Cuisinart ice cream maker and churn for 20-25 minutes.

Transfer to an airtight container and freeze for at least 2 hours before serving.

Matcha Green Tea Frozen Yogurt

Servings: 6-8

Ingredients

4 cups plain Greek yogurt

3/4 cup sugar

2 tablespoons matcha green tea powder

1 teaspoon vanilla extract

Instructions

Whisk together yogurt, sugar, matcha powder, and vanilla extract until smooth.

Chill the mixture in the refrigerator for at least 2 hours.

Pour the chilled mixture into the Cuisinart ice cream maker and churn for 20-25 minutes.

Transfer to an airtight container and freeze for at least 2 hours before serving.

Pomegranate Frozen Yogurt

Servings: 6-8

Ingredients

4 cups plain Greek yogurt

3/4 cup pomegranate juice

3/4 cup sugar

1/2 cup pomegranate seeds

Instructions

Whisk together yogurt, pomegranate juice, and sugar until the sugar is dissolved.

Stir in the pomegranate seeds.

Chill the mixture in the refrigerator for at least 2 hours.

Pour the chilled mixture into the Cuisinart ice cream maker and churn for 20-25 minutes.

Transfer to an airtight container and freeze for at least 2 hours before serving.

Black Cherry Frozen Yogurt

Servings: 6-8

Ingredients

4 cups plain Greek yogurt

3/4 cup sugar

2 cups black cherries, pitted and halved

1 teaspoon vanilla extract

Instructions

Puree the cherries and sugar in a blender until smooth. Mix the cherry puree with yogurt and vanilla extract. Chill the mixture in the refrigerator for at least 2 hours.

Pour the chilled mixture into the Cuisinart ice cream maker and churn for 20-25 minutes.

Transfer to an airtight container and freeze for at least 2 hours before serving.

Pear and Ginger Frozen Yogurt

Servings: 6-8

Ingredients

4 cups plain Greek yogurt

3/4 cup sugar

2 cups pear puree (about 4 pears)

1 tablespoon fresh grated ginger

Instructions

Puree the pears and sugar in a blender until smooth. Mix the pear puree with yogurt and grated ginger. Chill the mixture in the refrigerator for at least 2 hours.

Pour the chilled mixture into the Cuisinart ice cream maker and churn for 20-25 minutes.

Transfer to an airtight container and freeze for at least 2 hours before serving.

Fig Frozen Yogurt

Servings: 6-8

Ingredients

4 cups plain Greek yogurt

3/4 cup sugar

2 cups fig puree (about 8 figs)

1 teaspoon vanilla extract

Instructions

Puree the figs and sugar in a blender until smooth.

Mix the fig puree with yogurt and vanilla extract.

Chill the mixture in the refrigerator for at least 2 hours.

Pour the chilled mixture into the Cuisinart ice cream maker and churn for 20-25 minutes.

Transfer to an airtight container and freeze for at least 2 hours before serving.

Lychee Frozen Yogurt

Servings: 6-8

Ingredients

4 cups plain Greek yogurt

3/4 cup sugar

2 cups lychee puree (about 20 lychees)

Instructions

Puree the lychees and sugar in a blender until smooth. Mix the lychee puree with yogurt.

Chill the mixture in the refrigerator for at least 2 hours.

Pour the chilled mixture into the Cuisinart ice cream maker and churn for 20-25 minutes.

Transfer to an airtight container and freeze for at least 2 hours before serving.

Avocado Lime Frozen Yogurt

Servings: 6-8

Ingredients

4 cups plain Greek yogurt

3 ripe avocados, peeled and pitted

1 cup sugar

1/2 cup fresh lime juice

1 tablespoon lime zest

Instructions

Puree the avocados, sugar, lime juice, and lime zest in a blender until smooth.

Mix the avocado puree with yogurt. Chill the mixture in the refrigerator for at least 2 hours.

Pour the chilled mixture into the Cuisinart ice cream maker and churn for 20-25 minutes.

Transfer to an airtight container and freeze for at least 2 hours before serving.

Apple Cinnamon Frozen Yogurt

Servings: 6-8

Ingredients

4 cups plain Greek yogurt

2 cups applesauce

3/4 cup sugar

1 teaspoon cinnamon

1/2 teaspoon nutmeg

Instructions

Mix the yogurt, applesauce, sugar, cinnamon, and nutmeg in a bowl until smooth.

Chill the mixture in the refrigerator for at least 2 hours.

Pour the chilled mixture into the Cuisinart ice cream maker and churn for 20-25 minutes.

Transfer to an airtight container and freeze for at least 2 hours before serving.

Cucumber Mint Frozen Yogurt

Servings: 6-8

Ingredients

4 cups plain Greek yogurt

3/4 cup sugar

2 cucumbers, peeled and pureed

2 tablespoons fresh mint, chopped

1 tablespoon lemon juice

Instructions

Puree the cucumbers and sugar in a blender until smooth.

Mix the cucumber puree with yogurt, mint, and lemon juice.

Chill the mixture in the refrigerator for at least 2 hours.

Pour the chilled mixture into the Cuisinart ice cream maker and churn for 20-25 minutes.

Transfer to an airtight container and freeze for at least 2 hours before serving.

Pumpkin Spice Frozen Yogurt

Servings: 6-8

Ingredients

4 cups plain Greek yogurt

1 cup pumpkin puree

3/4 cup sugar

1 teaspoon cinnamon

1/2 teaspoon nutmeg

1/2 teaspoon ginger

1/2 teaspoon allspice

Instructions

Mix the yogurt, pumpkin puree, sugar, cinnamon, nutmeg, ginger, and allspice in a bowl until smooth.

Chill the mixture in the refrigerator for at least 2 hours.

Pour the chilled mixture into the Cuisinart ice cream maker and churn for 20-25 minutes.

Transfer to an airtight container and freeze for at least 2 hours before serving.

Mango Frozen Yogurt

Servings: 6-8

Ingredients

4 cups plain Greek yogurt

2 cups mango puree

3/4 cup sugar

Instructions

Blend the mango puree and sugar until the sugar is dissolved.

Mix the mango mixture with yogurt. Chill the mixture in the refrigerator for at least 2 hours.

Pour the chilled mixture into the Cuisinart ice cream maker and churn for 20-25 minutes.

Transfer to an airtight container and freeze for at least 2 hours before serving.

Basil Lemon Frozen Yogurt

Servings: 6-8

Ingredients

4 cups plain Greek yogurt

3/4 cup sugar

1/2 cup fresh lemon juice

1 tablespoon lemon zest

1/4 cup fresh basil leaves, finely chopped

Instructions

Whisk together the yogurt, sugar, lemon juice, lemon zest, and basil until the sugar is dissolved.

Chill the mixture in the refrigerator for at least 2 hours.

Pour the chilled mixture into the Cuisinart ice cream maker and churn for 20-25 minutes.

Transfer to an airtight container and freeze for at least 2 hours before serving.

Cardamom Orange Frozen Yogurt

Servings: 6-8

Ingredients

4 cups plain Greek yogurt

3/4 cup sugar

1/2 cup fresh orange juice

1 tablespoon orange zest

1/2 teaspoon ground cardamom

Instructions

Whisk together the yogurt, sugar, orange juice, orange zest, and cardamom until the sugar is dissolved.

Chill the mixture in the refrigerator for at least 2 hours.

Pour the chilled mixture into the Cuisinart ice cream maker and churn for 20-25 minutes.

Transfer to an airtight container and freeze for at least 2 hours before serving.

Sweet Corn Frozen Yogurt

Servings: 6-8

Ingredients

4 cups plain Greek yogurt

3/4 cup sugar

2 cups fresh corn kernels (about 4 ears of corn)

1 tablespoon honey

Instructions

Blend the corn kernels, sugar, and honey in a blender until smooth.

Mix the corn puree with yogurt.

Chill the mixture in the refrigerator for at least 2 hours.

Pour the chilled mixture into the Cuisinart ice cream maker and churn for 20-25 minutes.

Transfer to an airtight container and freeze for at least 2 hours before serving.

Chai Spiced Frozen Yogurt

Servings: 6-8

Ingredients

4 cups plain Greek yogurt

3/4 cup sugar

1/2 teaspoon ground cinnamon

1/2 teaspoon ground ginger

1/4 teaspoon ground cloves

1/4 teaspoon ground cardamom

1/4 teaspoon ground black pepper

Instructions

Whisk together the yogurt, sugar, and spices until the sugar is dissolved.

Chill the mixture in the refrigerator for at least 2 hours.

Pour the chilled mixture into the Cuisinart ice cream maker and churn for 20-25 minutes.

Transfer to an airtight container and freeze for at least 2 hours before serving.

3. Sorbet & Sherbet Recipes

Hibiscus Lime Sorbet

Servings: 6-8

Ingredients

4 cups water

1 cup dried hibiscus flowers

1 cup sugar

1/2 cup fresh lime juice

1 tablespoon lime zest

Instructions

Bring water to a boil, add hibiscus flowers, and steep for 10 minutes.

Strain the hibiscus tea into a bowl, discarding the flowers.

Stir in sugar until dissolved, then add lime juice and lime zest.

Chill the mixture in the refrigerator for at least 2 hours.

Pour the chilled mixture into the Cuisinart ice cream maker and churn for 20-25 minutes.

Transfer to an airtight container and freeze for at least 2 hours before serving.

Cucumber Mint Sorbet

Servings: 6-8

Ingredients

4 cups cucumber, peeled and chopped

1 cup sugar

1 cup water

1/4 cup fresh mint leaves

2 tablespoons lemon juice

Instructions

Puree cucumber and mint in a blender until smooth.

In a saucepan, combine water and sugar, bring to a boil until sugar is dissolved, then let cool.

Mix the cucumber puree with the cooled syrup and lemon juice.

Chill the mixture in the refrigerator for at least 2 hours.

Pour the chilled mixture into the Cuisinart ice cream maker and churn for 20-25 minutes.

Transfer to an airtight container and freeze for at least 2 hours before serving.

Grapefruit Campari Sorbet

Servings: 6-8

Ingredients

3 cups fresh grapefruit juice

1 cup sugar

1/4 cup Campari

1 tablespoon grapefruit zest

Instructions

In a saucepan, combine grapefruit juice, sugar, and zest. Heat until sugar is dissolved. Let cool.

Stir in Campari.

Chill the mixture in the refrigerator for at least 2 hours.

Pour the chilled mixture into the Cuisinart ice cream maker and churn for 20-25 minutes.

Transfer to an airtight container and freeze for at least 2 hours before serving.

Coconut Lemongrass Sorbet

Servings: 6-8

Ingredients

3 cups coconut milk

1 cup water

1 cup sugar

3 stalks lemongrass, chopped

2 tablespoons lime juice

Instructions

In a saucepan, combine coconut milk, water, sugar, and lemongrass. Simmer for 10 minutes, then let steep for 20 minutes.

Strain the mixture, discarding lemongrass.

Add lime juice to the strained mixture.

Chill the mixture in the refrigerator for at least 2 hours.

Pour the chilled mixture into the Cuisinart ice cream maker and churn for 20-25 minutes.

Transfer to an airtight container and freeze for at least 2 hours before serving.

Spiced Apple Cider Sorbet

Servings: 6-8

Ingredients

4 cups apple cider

1 cup sugar

1 cinnamon stick

4 whole cloves

1 tablespoon lemon juice

Instructions

In a saucepan, combine apple cider, sugar, cinnamon stick, and cloves. Heat until sugar is dissolved, then let steep for 10 minutes. Remove spices.

Add lemon juice to the mixture.

Chill the mixture in the refrigerator for at least 2 hours.

Pour the chilled mixture into the Cuisinart ice cream maker and churn for 20-25 minutes.

Transfer to an airtight container and freeze for at least 2 hours before serving.

Pear Ginger Sorbet

Servings: 6-8

Ingredients

4 cups pear puree (about 6 pears, peeled and blended)

1 cup sugar

1 cup water

1 tablespoon fresh grated ginger

1 tablespoon lemon juice

Instructions

In a saucepan, combine water, sugar, and grated ginger. Bring to a boil until sugar is dissolved, then let cool.

Mix the pear puree with the cooled syrup and lemon juice.

Chill the mixture in the refrigerator for at least 2 hours.

Pour the chilled mixture into the Cuisinart ice cream maker and churn for 20-25 minutes.

Transfer to an airtight container and freeze for at least 2 hours before serving.

Blueberry Lavender Sorbet

Servings: 6-8

Ingredients

4 cups fresh blueberries

1 cup sugar

1 cup water

1 tablespoon dried lavender

2 tablespoons lemon juice

Instructions

In a blender, puree blueberries until smooth.

In a saucepan, combine water, sugar, and lavender. Bring to a boil until sugar is dissolved, then let steep for 10 minutes. Strain the mixture.

Mix the blueberry puree with the lavender syrup and lemon juice.

Chill the mixture in the refrigerator for at least 2 hours.

Pour the chilled mixture into the Cuisinart ice cream maker and churn for 20-25 minutes.

Transfer to an airtight container and freeze for at least 2 hours before serving.

Tomato Basil Sorbet

Servings: 6-8

Ingredients

4 cups ripe tomatoes, chopped

1 cup sugar

1 cup water

1/4 cup fresh basil leaves, chopped

2 tablespoons lemon juice

Instructions

In a blender, puree tomatoes until smooth. Strain to remove seeds and skins.

In a saucepan, combine water and sugar. Bring to a boil until sugar is dissolved, then let cool.

Mix the tomato puree with the cooled syrup, basil, and lemon juice.

Chill the mixture in the refrigerator for at least 2 hours.

Pour the chilled mixture into the Cuisinart ice cream maker and churn for 20-25 minutes.

Transfer to an airtight container and freeze for at least 2 hours before serving.

Passion Fruit Sorbet

Servings: 6-8

Ingredients

2 cups passion fruit pulp (about 12-15 passion fruits)

1 cup sugar

1 cup water

1 tablespoon lemon juice

Instructions

Scoop out the pulp from the passion fruits and strain to remove seeds.

In a saucepan, combine water and sugar. Bring to a boil until sugar is dissolved, then let cool.

Mix the passion fruit pulp with the cooled syrup and lemon juice.

Chill the mixture in the refrigerator for at least 2 hours.

Pour the chilled mixture into the Cuisinart ice cream maker and churn for 20-25 minutes.

Transfer to an airtight container and freeze for at least 2 hours before serving.

Lemon Sorbet

Servings: 6-8

Ingredients

2 cups water

1 cup sugar

1 cup fresh lemon juice

1 tablespoon lemon zest

Instructions

In a saucepan, combine water and sugar. Bring to a boil, stirring until sugar is dissolved. Remove from heat and let cool.

Add lemon juice and zest to the cooled syrup.

Chill the mixture in the refrigerator for at least 2 hours.

Pour the chilled mixture into the Cuisinart ice cream maker and churn for 20-25 minutes.

Transfer to an airtight container and freeze for at least 2 hours before serving.

Strawberry Basil Sorbet

Servings: 6-8

Ingredients

4 cups fresh strawberries, hulled

1 cup sugar

1 cup water

1 tablespoon lemon juice

1/4 cup fresh basil leaves, chopped

Instructions

In a blender, puree strawberries until smooth. Strain to remove seeds if desired.

In a saucepan, combine water and sugar. Bring to a boil, stirring until sugar is dissolved. Remove from heat and let cool.

Mix the strawberry puree, lemon juice, basil leaves, and cooled syrup.

Chill the mixture in the refrigerator for at least 2 hours.

Pour the chilled mixture into the Cuisinart ice cream maker and churn for 20-25 minutes.

Transfer to an airtight container and freeze for at least 2 hours before serving.

Peach Sorbet

Servings: 6-8

Ingredients

4 cups ripe peach slices

1 cup sugar

1 cup water

2 tablespoons lemon juice

Instructions

In a blender, puree peach slices until smooth.

In a saucepan, combine water and sugar. Bring to a boil, stirring until sugar is dissolved. Remove from heat and let cool.

Mix the peach puree, lemon juice, and cooled syrup.

Chill the mixture in the refrigerator for at least 2 hours.

Pour the chilled mixture into the Cuisinart ice cream maker and churn for 20-25 minutes.

Transfer to an airtight container and freeze for at least 2 hours before serving.

Blueberry Sorbet

Servings: 6-8

Ingredients

4 cups fresh blueberries

1 cup sugar

1 cup water

2 tablespoons lemon juice

Instructions

In a blender, puree blueberries until smooth. Strain to remove skins if desired.

In a saucepan, combine water and sugar. Bring to a boil, stirring until sugar is dissolved. Remove from heat and let cool.

Mix the blueberry puree, lemon juice, and cooled syrup.

Chill the mixture in the refrigerator for at least 2 hours.

Pour the chilled mixture into the Cuisinart ice cream maker and churn for 20-25 minutes.

Transfer to an airtight container and freeze for at least 2 hours before serving.

Coconut Lime Sorbet

Servings: 6-8

Ingredients

1 cup coconut milk

1 cup water

1 cup sugar

1/2 cup fresh lime juice

1 tablespoon lime zest

Instructions

In a saucepan, combine coconut milk, water, and sugar. Bring to a boil, stirring until sugar is dissolved. Remove from heat and let cool.

Add lime juice and lime zest to the cooled mixture.

Chill the mixture in the refrigerator for at least 2 hours.

Pour the chilled mixture into the Cuisinart ice cream maker and churn for 20-25 minutes.

Transfer to an airtight container and freeze for at least 2 hours before serving.

Cantaloupe Sorbet

Servings: 6-8

Ingredients

4 cups cantaloupe chunks

1 cup sugar

1 cup water

2 tablespoons lemon juice

Instructions

In a blender, puree cantaloupe chunks until smooth.

In a saucepan, combine water and sugar. Bring to a boil, stirring until sugar is dissolved. Remove from heat and let cool.

Mix the cantaloupe puree, lemon juice, and cooled syrup.

Chill the mixture in the refrigerator for at least 2 hours.

Pour the chilled mixture into the Cuisinart ice cream maker and churn for 20-25 minutes.

Transfer to an airtight container and freeze for at least 2 hours before serving.

Orange Sherbet

Servings: 6-8

Ingredients

2 cups fresh orange juice

1 cup sugar

1 cup milk

1 tablespoon orange zest

1 tablespoon lemon juice

Instructions

In a bowl, combine orange juice, sugar, milk, orange zest, and lemon juice. Stir until the sugar is dissolved.

Chill the mixture in the refrigerator for at least 2 hours.

Pour the chilled mixture into the Cuisinart ice cream maker and churn for 20-25 minutes.

Transfer to an airtight container and freeze for at least 2 hours before serving.

Blackberry Sorbet

Servings: 6-8

Ingredients

4 cups blackberries

1 cup sugar

1/2 cup water

1 tablespoon lemon juice

Instructions

Puree blackberries and strain to remove seeds.

Combine sugar and water in a saucepan and heat until sugar dissolves. Cool the syrup.

Mix syrup with blackberry puree and lemon juice. Chill the mixture.

Churn in the ice cream maker for 20-25 minutes. Freeze for at least 2 hours.

Papaya Sorbet

Servings: 6-8

Ingredients

4 cups papaya puree

1 cup sugar

1/2 cup water

1 tablespoon lime juice

Instructions

Combine sugar and water in a saucepan and heat until sugar dissolves. Cool the syrup.

Mix syrup with papaya puree and lime juice. Chill the mixture.

Churn in the ice cream maker for 20-25 minutes. Freeze for at least 2 hours.

Pineapple Coconut Sherbet

Servings: 6-8

Ingredients

2 cups pineapple juice

1 cup coconut milk

1 cup sugar

1 tablespoon lemon juice

Instructions

In a bowl, combine pineapple juice, coconut milk, sugar, and lemon juice. Stir until the sugar is dissolved.

Chill the mixture in the refrigerator for at least 2 hours.

Pour the chilled mixture into the Cuisinart ice cream maker and churn for 20-25 minutes.

Transfer to an airtight container and freeze for at least 2 hours before serving.

Mango Lime Sherbet

Servings: 6-8

Ingredients

2 cups fresh mango puree (from 3-4 ripe mangoes)

1 cup sugar

1 cup milk

1/4 cup fresh lime juice

1 tablespoon lime zest

Instructions

In a bowl, combine mango puree, sugar, milk, lime juice, and lime zest. Stir until the sugar is dissolved.

Chill the mixture in the refrigerator for at least 2 hours.

Pour the chilled mixture into the Cuisinart ice cream maker and churn for 20-25 minutes.

Transfer to an airtight container and freeze for at least 2 hours before serving.

Raspberry Lemon Sherbet

Servings: 6-8

Ingredients

2 cups fresh raspberries

1 cup sugar

1 cup milk

1 cup water

1/4 cup fresh lemon juice

1 tablespoon lemon zest

Instructions

In a blender, puree raspberries until smooth. Strain to remove seeds.

In a bowl, combine raspberry puree, sugar, milk, water, lemon juice, and lemon zest. Stir until the sugar is dissolved.

Chill the mixture in the refrigerator for at least 2 hours.

Pour the chilled mixture into the Cuisinart ice cream maker and churn for 20-25 minutes.

Transfer to an airtight container and freeze for at least 2 hours before serving.

Peach Ginger Sherbet

Servings: 6-8

Ingredients

2 cups fresh peach puree (from 4-5 ripe peaches)

1 cup sugar

1 cup milk

1/2 cup water

1 tablespoon fresh grated ginger

1 tablespoon lemon juice

Instructions

In a bowl, combine peach puree, sugar, milk, water, grated ginger, and lemon juice. Stir until the sugar is dissolved.

Chill the mixture in the refrigerator for at least 2 hours.

Pour the chilled mixture into the Cuisinart ice cream maker and churn for 20-25 minutes.

Transfer to an airtight container and freeze for at least 2 hours before serving.

Grapefruit Mint Sherbet

Servings: 6-8

Ingredients

2 cups fresh grapefruit juice

1 cup sugar

1 cup milk

1/2 cup water

1/4 cup fresh mint leaves, chopped

1 tablespoon grapefruit zest

Instructions

In a bowl, combine grapefruit juice, sugar, milk, water, mint leaves, and grapefruit zest. Stir until the sugar is dissolved.

Chill the mixture in the refrigerator for at least 2 hours.

Pour the chilled mixture into the Cuisinart ice cream maker and churn for 20-25 minutes.

Transfer to an airtight container and freeze for at least 2 hours before serving.

Lemon Thyme Sherbet

Servings: 6-8

Ingredients

2 cups fresh lemon juice

1 cup sugar

1 cup milk

1/2 cup water

1 tablespoon fresh thyme leaves

1 tablespoon lemon zest

Instructions

In a bowl, combine lemon juice, sugar, milk, water, thyme leaves, and lemon zest. Stir until the sugar is dissolved.

Chill the mixture in the refrigerator for at least 2 hours.

Pour the chilled mixture into the Cuisinart ice cream maker and churn for 20-25 minutes.

Transfer to an airtight container and freeze for at least 2 hours before serving.

Kiwi Lime Sherbet

Servings: 6-8

Ingredients

2 cups fresh kiwi puree (from 6-8 ripe kiwis)

1 cup sugar

1 cup milk

1/4 cup fresh lime juice

1 tablespoon lime zest

Instructions

In a bowl, combine kiwi puree, sugar, milk, lime juice, and lime zest. Stir until the sugar is dissolved.

Chill the mixture in the refrigerator for at least 2 hours.

Pour the chilled mixture into the Cuisinart ice cream maker and churn for 20-25 minutes.

Transfer to an airtight container and freeze for at least 2 hours before serving.

4. Gelato Recipes

Vanilla Bean Gelato

Servings: 6-8

Ingredients

2 cups whole milk

1 cup heavy cream

3/4 cup sugar

1 vanilla bean, split and scraped

5 large egg yolks

Instructions

In a saucepan, combine milk, cream, and vanilla bean seeds and pod. Heat until just simmering, then remove from heat and let steep for 30 minutes.

In a bowl, whisk together egg yolks and sugar until pale and thick.

Remove vanilla pod from milk mixture, then slowly whisk the warm milk into the egg mixture.

Return mixture to saucepan and cook over medium heat, stirring constantly, until it thickens and coats the back of a spoon.

Strain the mixture into a bowl and chill in the refrigerator for at least 4 hours.

Pour the chilled mixture into the Cuisinart ice cream maker and churn for 25-30 minutes.

Transfer to an airtight container and freeze for at least 2 hours before serving.

Chocolate Hazelnut Gelato

Servings: 6-8

Ingredients

2 cups whole milk

1 cup heavy cream

3/4 cup sugar

1/2 cup cocoa powder

5 large egg yolks

1/2 cup hazelnut spread (e.g., Nutella)

Instructions

In a saucepan, combine milk, cream, sugar, and cocoa powder. Heat until just simmering, stirring until sugar and cocoa are dissolved.

In a bowl, whisk together egg yolks until pale and thick.

Slowly whisk the warm milk mixture into the egg yolks.

Return mixture to saucepan and cook over medium heat, stirring constantly, until it thickens and coats the back of a spoon.

Remove from heat and whisk in the hazelnut spread until smooth.

Strain the mixture into a bowl and chill in the refrigerator for at least 4 hours.

Pour the chilled mixture into the Cuisinart ice cream maker and churn for 25-30 minutes.

Transfer to an airtight container and freeze for at least 2 hours before serving.

Pistachio Gelato

Servings: 6-8

Ingredients

2 cups whole milk

1 cup heavy cream

3/4 cup sugar

1 cup shelled pistachios

5 large egg yolks

Instructions

In a blender, grind pistachios until finely ground.

In a saucepan, combine milk, cream, and ground pistachios. Heat until just simmering, then remove from heat and let steep for 30 minutes.

In a bowl, whisk together egg yolks and sugar until pale and thick.

Slowly whisk the warm milk mixture into the egg yolks.

Return mixture to saucepan and cook over medium heat, stirring constantly, until it thickens and coats the back of a spoon.

Strain the mixture into a bowl and chill in the refrigerator for at least 4 hours.

Pour the chilled mixture into the Cuisinart ice cream maker and churn for 25-30 minutes.

Transfer to an airtight container and freeze for at least 2 hours before serving.

Strawberry Gelato

Servings: 6-8

Ingredients

2 cups fresh strawberries, hulled and pureed

1 cup whole milk

1 cup heavy cream

3/4 cup sugar

5 large egg yolks

1 tablespoon lemon juice

Instructions

In a saucepan, combine milk, cream, and half of the sugar. Heat until just simmering, then remove from heat.

In a bowl, whisk together egg yolks and remaining sugar until pale and thick.

Slowly whisk the warm milk mixture into the egg yolks.

Return mixture to saucepan and cook over medium heat, stirring constantly, until it thickens and coats the back of a spoon.

Remove from heat and stir in strawberry puree and lemon juice.

Chill the mixture in the refrigerator for at least 4 hours.

Pour the chilled mixture into the Cuisinart ice cream maker and churn for 25-30 minutes.

Transfer to an airtight container and freeze for at least 2 hours before serving.

Coffee Gelato

Servings: 6-8

Ingredients

2 cups whole milk

1 cup heavy cream

3/4 cup sugar

3 tablespoons instant espresso powder

5 large egg yolks

Instructions

In a saucepan, combine milk, cream, sugar, and espresso powder. Heat until just simmering, stirring until sugar and espresso are dissolved.

In a bowl, whisk together egg yolks until pale and thick.

Slowly whisk the warm milk mixture into the egg yolks.

Return mixture to saucepan and cook over medium heat, stirring constantly, until it thickens and coats the back of a spoon.

Strain the mixture into a bowl and chill in the refrigerator for at least 4 hours.

Pour the chilled mixture into the Cuisinart ice cream maker and churn for 25-30 minutes.

Transfer to an airtight container and freeze for at least 2 hours before serving.

Lemon Gelato

Servings: 6-8

Ingredients

2 cups whole milk

1 cup heavy cream

3/4 cup sugar

Zest of 2 lemons

5 large egg yolks

1/2 cup fresh lemon juice

Instructions

In a saucepan, combine milk, cream, sugar, and lemon zest. Heat until just simmering, then remove from heat and let steep for 30 minutes.

In a bowl, whisk together egg yolks until pale and thick.

Slowly whisk the warm milk mixture into the egg yolks.

Return mixture to saucepan and cook over medium heat, stirring constantly, until it thickens and coats the back of a spoon.

Remove from heat and stir in lemon juice.

Strain the mixture into a bowl and chill in the refrigerator for at least 4 hours.

Pour the chilled mixture into the Cuisinart ice cream maker and churn for 25-30 minutes.

Transfer to an airtight container and freeze for at least 2 hours before serving.

Coconut Gelato

Servings: 6-8

Ingredients

2 cups whole milk

1 cup coconut milk

3/4 cup sugar

1/2 cup shredded coconut

5 large egg yolks

Instructions

In a saucepan, combine milk, coconut milk, sugar, and shredded coconut. Heat until just simmering, then remove from heat and let steep for 30 minutes.

In a bowl, whisk together egg yolks until pale and thick.

Slowly whisk the warm milk mixture into the egg yolks.

Return mixture to saucepan and cook over medium heat, stirring constantly, until it thickens and coats the back of a spoon.

Strain the mixture into a bowl and chill in the refrigerator for at least 4 hours.

Pour the chilled mixture into the Cuisinart ice cream maker and churn for 25-30 minutes.

Transfer to an airtight container and freeze for at least 2 hours before serving.

Maple Walnut Gelato

Servings: 6-8

Ingredients

2 cups whole milk

1 cup heavy cream

1/2 cup maple syrup

1/4 cup sugar

5 large egg yolks

1/2 cup chopped walnuts, toasted

Instructions

In a saucepan, combine milk, cream, maple syrup, and sugar. Heat until just simmering, then remove from heat.

In a bowl, whisk together egg yolks until pale and thick.

Slowly whisk the warm milk mixture into the egg yolks.

Return mixture to saucepan and cook over medium heat, stirring constantly, until it thickens and coats the back of a spoon.

Strain the mixture into a bowl and chill in the refrigerator for at least 4 hours.

Pour the chilled mixture into the Cuisinart ice cream maker and churn for 25-30 minutes. During the last 5 minutes of churning, add the chopped walnuts.

Transfer to an airtight container and freeze for at least 2 hours before serving.

Banana Gelato

Servings: 6-8

Ingredients

2 ripe bananas, mashed

2 cups whole milk

1 cup heavy cream

3/4 cup sugar

5 large egg yolks

1 tablespoon lemon juice

Instructions

In a saucepan, combine milk, cream, and sugar. Heat until just simmering, then remove from heat.

In a bowl, whisk together egg yolks until pale and thick.

Slowly whisk the warm milk mixture into the egg yolks.

Return mixture to saucepan and cook over medium heat, stirring constantly, until it thickens and coats the back of a spoon.

Remove from heat and stir in mashed bananas and lemon juice.

Chill the mixture in the refrigerator for at least 4 hours.

Pour the chilled mixture into the Cuisinart ice cream maker and churn for 25-30 minutes.

Transfer to an airtight container and freeze for at least 2 hours before serving.

Cinnamon Gelato

Servings: 6-8

Ingredients

2 cups whole milk

1 cup heavy cream

3/4 cup sugar

1 tablespoon ground cinnamon

5 large egg yolks

Instructions

In a saucepan, combine milk, cream, sugar, and cinnamon. Heat until just simmering, stirring until sugar is dissolved.

In a bowl, whisk together egg yolks until pale and thick.

Slowly whisk the warm milk mixture into the egg yolks.

Return mixture to saucepan and cook over medium heat, stirring constantly, until it thickens and coats the back of a spoon.

Strain the mixture into a bowl and chill in the refrigerator for at least 4 hours.

Pour the chilled mixture into the Cuisinart ice cream maker and churn for 25-30 minutes.

Transfer to an airtight container and freeze for at least 2 hours before serving.

Honey Lavender Gelato

Servings: 6-8

Ingredients

2 cups whole milk

1 cup heavy cream

1/2 cup honey

1/4 cup sugar

1 tablespoon dried lavender

5 large egg yolks

Instructions

In a saucepan, combine milk, cream, honey, sugar, and lavender. Heat until just simmering, then remove from heat and let steep for 30 minutes. Strain to remove lavender.

In a bowl, whisk together egg yolks until pale and thick.

Slowly whisk the warm milk mixture into the egg yolks.

Return mixture to saucepan and cook over medium heat, stirring constantly, until it thickens and coats the back of a spoon.

Strain the mixture into a bowl and chill in the refrigerator for at least 4 hours.

Pour the chilled mixture into the Cuisinart ice cream maker and churn for 25-30 minutes.

Transfer to an airtight container and freeze for at least 2 hours before serving.

Matcha Green Tea Gelato

Servings: 6-8

Ingredients

2 cups whole milk

1 cup heavy cream

3/4 cup sugar

2 tablespoons matcha green tea powder

5 large egg yolks

Instructions

In a saucepan, combine milk, cream, and sugar. Heat until just simmering, then remove from heat.

In a bowl, whisk together egg yolks until pale and thick.

Dissolve matcha powder in a small amount of the warm milk mixture, then whisk into the egg yolks.

Slowly whisk the remaining warm milk mixture into the egg yolks.

Return mixture to saucepan and cook over medium heat, stirring constantly, until it thickens and coats the back of a spoon.

Strain the mixture into a bowl and chill in the refrigerator for at least 4 hours.

Pour the chilled mixture into the Cuisinart ice cream maker and churn for 25-30 minutes.

Transfer to an airtight container and freeze for at least 2 hours before serving.

Honey Fig Gelato

Servings: 6-8

Ingredients

2 cups whole milk

1 cup heavy cream

1/2 cup honey

1/4 cup sugar

1 cup fresh figs, pureed

5 large egg yolks

Instructions

In a saucepan, combine milk, cream, honey, and sugar. Heat until just simmering, then remove from heat.

In a bowl, whisk together egg yolks until pale and thick.

Slowly whisk the warm milk mixture into the egg yolks.

Return mixture to saucepan and cook over medium heat, stirring constantly, until it thickens and coats the back of a spoon.

Remove from heat and stir in pureed figs.

Chill the mixture in the refrigerator for at least 4 hours.

Pour the chilled mixture into the Cuisinart ice cream maker and churn for 25-30 minutes.

Transfer to an airtight container and freeze for at least 2 hours before serving.

Tiramisu Gelato

Servings: 6-8

Ingredients

2 cups whole milk

1 cup heavy cream

3/4 cup sugar

3 tablespoons instant espresso powder

1/4 cup mascarpone cheese

5 large egg yolks

1/4 cup coffee liqueur (optional)

1 tablespoon cocoa powder

Instructions

In a saucepan, combine milk, cream, sugar, and espresso powder. Heat until just simmering, stirring until sugar and espresso are dissolved.

In a bowl, whisk together egg yolks until pale and thick.

Slowly whisk the warm milk mixture into the egg yolks.

Return mixture to saucepan and cook over medium heat, stirring constantly, until it thickens and coats the back of a spoon.

Remove from heat and whisk in mascarpone cheese and coffee liqueur.

Chill the mixture in the refrigerator for at least 4 hours.

Pour the chilled mixture into the Cuisinart ice cream maker and churn for 25-30 minutes.

Transfer to an airtight container, dust with cocoa powder, and freeze for at least 2 hours before serving.

Black Sesame Gelato

Servings: 6-8

Ingredients

2 cups whole milk

1 cup heavy cream

3/4 cup sugar

1/4 cup black sesame seeds, toasted and ground

5 large egg yolks

Instructions

In a saucepan, combine milk, cream, sugar, and ground black sesame seeds. Heat until just simmering, then remove from heat.

In a bowl, whisk together egg yolks until pale and thick.

Slowly whisk the warm milk mixture into the egg yolks.

Return mixture to saucepan and cook over medium heat, stirring constantly, until it thickens and coats the back of a spoon.

Strain the mixture into a bowl and chill in the refrigerator for at least 4 hours.

Pour the chilled mixture into the Cuisinart ice cream maker and churn for 25-30 minutes.

Transfer to an airtight container and freeze for at least 2 hours before serving.

Dark Chocolate Orange Gelato

Servings: 6-8

Ingredients

2 cups whole milk

1 cup heavy cream

3/4 cup sugar

1/2 cup cocoa powder

1 tablespoon orange zest

5 large egg yolks

1/2 cup dark chocolate, finely chopped

Instructions

In a saucepan, combine milk, cream, sugar, cocoa powder, and orange zest. Heat until just simmering, stirring until sugar and cocoa are dissolved.

In a bowl, whisk together egg yolks until pale and thick.

Slowly whisk the warm milk mixture into the egg yolks.

Return mixture to saucepan and cook over medium heat, stirring constantly, until it thickens and coats the back of a spoon.

Remove from heat and stir in chopped dark chocolate until melted.

Strain the mixture into a bowl and chill in the refrigerator for at least 4 hours.

Pour the chilled mixture into the Cuisinart ice cream maker and churn for 25-30 minutes.

Transfer to an airtight container and freeze for at least 2 hours before serving.

Caramel Apple Gelato

Servings: 6-8

Ingredients

2 cups whole milk

1 cup heavy cream

3/4 cup sugar

1/2 cup caramel sauce

1 cup applesauce

5 large egg yolks

1 teaspoon cinnamon

Instructions

In a saucepan, combine milk, cream, sugar, and caramel sauce. Heat until just simmering, then remove from heat.

In a bowl, whisk together egg yolks until pale and thick.

Slowly whisk the warm milk mixture into the egg yolks.

Return mixture to saucepan and cook over medium heat, stirring constantly, until it thickens and coats the back of a spoon.

Remove from heat and stir in applesauce and cinnamon.

Chill the mixture in the refrigerator for at least 4 hours.

Pour the chilled mixture into the Cuisinart ice cream maker and churn for 25-30 minutes.

Transfer to an airtight container and freeze for at least 2 hours before serving.

Blueberry Cheesecake Gelato

Servings: 6-8

Ingredients

2 cups whole milk

1 cup heavy cream

3/4 cup sugar

1 cup fresh blueberries, pureed

1/2 cup cream cheese, softened

5 large egg yolks

1 tablespoon lemon juice

Instructions

In a saucepan, combine milk, cream, and half of the sugar. Heat until just simmering, then remove from heat.

In a bowl, whisk together egg yolks and remaining sugar until pale and thick.

Slowly whisk the warm milk mixture into the egg yolks.

Return mixture to saucepan and cook over medium heat, stirring constantly, until it thickens and coats the back of a spoon.

Remove from heat and whisk in cream cheese until smooth. Stir in blueberry puree and lemon juice.

Chill the mixture in the refrigerator for at least 4 hours.

Pour the chilled mixture into the Cuisinart ice cream maker and churn for 25-30 minutes.

Transfer to an airtight container and freeze for at least 2 hours before serving.

Blood Orange Gelato

Servings: 6-8

Ingredients

2 cups whole milk

1 cup heavy cream

3/4 cup sugar

Zest of 2 blood oranges

1/2 cup fresh blood orange juice

5 large egg yolks

Instructions

In a saucepan, combine milk, cream, sugar, and blood orange zest. Heat until just simmering, then remove from heat and let steep for 30 minutes.

In a bowl, whisk together egg yolks until pale and thick.

Slowly whisk the warm milk mixture into the egg yolks.

Return mixture to saucepan and cook over medium heat, stirring constantly, until it thickens and coats the back of a spoon.

Remove from heat and stir in blood orange juice.

Chill the mixture in the refrigerator for at least 4 hours.

Pour the chilled mixture into the Cuisinart ice cream maker and churn for 25-30 minutes.

Transfer to an airtight container and freeze for at least 2 hours before serving.

Raspberry Gelato

Servings: 6-8

Ingredients

2 cups whole milk

1 cup heavy cream

3/4 cup sugar

2 cups fresh raspberries

1 tablespoon lemon juice

5 large egg yolks

Instructions

In a blender, puree raspberries with lemon juice. Strain to remove seeds if desired.

In a saucepan, combine milk, cream, and sugar. Heat until just simmering, then remove from heat.

In a bowl, whisk together egg yolks until pale and thick.

Slowly whisk the warm milk mixture into the egg yolks.

Return mixture to saucepan and cook over medium heat, stirring constantly, until it thickens and coats the back of a spoon.

Remove from heat and stir in raspberry puree.

Chill the mixture in the refrigerator for at least 4 hours.

Pour the chilled mixture into the Cuisinart ice cream maker and churn for 25-30 minutes.

Transfer to an airtight container and freeze for at least 2 hours before serving.

Chai Spice Gelato

Servings: 6-8

Ingredients

2 cups whole milk

1 cup heavy cream

3/4 cup sugar

2 tablespoons chai tea leaves or 4 chai tea bags

5 large egg yolks

Instructions

In a saucepan, combine milk, cream, sugar, and chai tea leaves. Heat until just simmering, then remove from heat and let steep for 15 minutes. Strain to remove tea leaves.

In a bowl, whisk together egg yolks until pale and thick.

Slowly whisk the warm milk mixture into the egg yolks.

Return mixture to saucepan and cook over medium heat, stirring constantly, until it thickens and coats the back of a spoon.

Chill the mixture in the refrigerator for at least 4 hours.

Pour the chilled mixture into the Cuisinart ice cream maker and churn for 25-30 minutes.

Transfer to an airtight container and freeze for at least 2 hours before serving.

Almond Fig Gelato

Servings: 6-8

Ingredients

2 cups whole milk

1 cup heavy cream

3/4 cup sugar

1 cup dried figs, chopped

1/2 teaspoon almond extract

5 large egg yolks

1/2 cup chopped almonds, toasted

Instructions

In a saucepan, combine milk, cream, sugar, and chopped figs. Heat until just simmering, then remove from heat and let steep for 30 minutes.

In a bowl, whisk together egg yolks until pale and thick.

Slowly whisk the warm milk mixture into the egg yolks.

Return mixture to saucepan and cook over medium heat, stirring constantly, until it thickens and coats the back of a spoon.

Remove from heat and stir in almond extract.

Chill the mixture in the refrigerator for at least 4 hours.

Pour the chilled mixture into the Cuisinart ice cream maker and churn for 25-30 minutes. During the last 5 minutes of churning, add toasted almonds.

Transfer to an airtight container and freeze for at least 2 hours before serving.

Lemon Thyme Gelato

Servings: 6-8

Ingredients

2 cups whole milk

1 cup heavy cream

3/4 cup sugar

Zest of 2 lemons

1/4 cup fresh lemon juice

1 tablespoon fresh thyme leaves

5 large egg yolks

Instructions

In a saucepan, combine milk, cream, sugar, lemon zest, and thyme leaves. Heat until just simmering, then remove from heat and let steep for 30 minutes. Strain to remove thyme leaves.

In a bowl, whisk together egg yolks until pale and thick.

Slowly whisk the warm milk mixture into the egg yolks.

Return mixture to saucepan and cook over medium heat, stirring constantly, until it thickens and coats the back of a spoon.

Remove from heat and stir in lemon juice.

Chill the mixture in the refrigerator for at least 4 hours.

Pour the chilled mixture into the Cuisinart ice cream maker and churn for 25-30 minutes.

Transfer to an airtight container and freeze for at least 2 hours before serving.

Ginger Pear Gelato

Servings: 6-8

Ingredients

2 cups whole milk

1 cup heavy cream

3/4 cup sugar

2 ripe pears, peeled and chopped

2 tablespoons fresh ginger, grated

5 large egg yolks

Instructions

In a saucepan, combine milk, cream, sugar, chopped pears, and grated ginger. Heat until just simmering, then remove from heat and let steep for 15 minutes.

In a blender, puree the mixture until smooth.

In a bowl, whisk together egg yolks until pale and thick.

Slowly whisk the warm milk mixture into the egg yolks.

Return mixture to saucepan and cook over medium heat, stirring constantly, until it thickens and coats the back of a spoon.

Chill the mixture in the refrigerator for at least 4 hours.

Pour the chilled mixture into the Cuisinart ice cream maker and churn for 25-30 minutes.

Transfer to an airtight container and freeze for at least 2 hours before serving.

5. Frosty Cocktails

Piña Colada Sorbet

Servings: 6-8

Ingredients

2 cups pineapple juice

1 cup coconut milk

1/2 cup rum

3/4 cup sugar

1/4 cup lime juice

Instructions

In a large bowl, combine pineapple juice, coconut milk, rum, sugar, and lime juice. Stir until sugar is dissolved.

Chill the mixture in the refrigerator for at least 2 hours.

Pour the chilled mixture into the Cuisinart ice cream maker and churn for 20-25 minutes.

Transfer to an airtight container and freeze for at least 2 hours before serving.

Margarita Sorbet

Servings: 6-8

Ingredients

2 cups water

1 cup sugar

1 cup fresh lime juice

1/2 cup tequila

1/4 cup triple sec

Instructions

In a saucepan, heat water and sugar until sugar is dissolved. Let cool.

In a large bowl, combine cooled sugar syrup, lime juice, tequila, and triple sec. Stir well.

Chill the mixture in the refrigerator for at least 2 hours. Pour the chilled mixture into the Cuisinart ice cream maker and churn for 20-25 minutes.

Transfer to an airtight container and freeze for at least 2 hours before serving.

Frozen Piña Colada

Servings: 6-8

Ingredients

2 cups pineapple chunks

1 cup coconut milk

1/2 cup rum

3/4 cup sugar

1/4 cup lime juice

Instructions

In a blender, puree pineapple chunks until smooth.

In a large bowl, combine pineapple puree, coconut milk, rum, sugar, and lime juice. Stir until sugar is dissolved. Chill the mixture in the refrigerator for at least 2 hours. Pour the chilled mixture into the Cuisinart ice cream maker and churn for 20-25 minutes.

Transfer to an airtight container and freeze for at least 2 hours before serving.

Strawberry Daiquiri Sorbet

Servings: 6-8

Ingredients

2 cups fresh strawberries, hulled and pureed

1 cup water

1/2 cup rum

3/4 cup sugar

1/4 cup lime juice

Instructions

In a large bowl, combine strawberry puree, water, rum, sugar, and lime juice. Stir until sugar is dissolved.

Chill the mixture in the refrigerator for at least 2 hours.

Pour the chilled mixture into the Cuisinart ice cream maker and churn for 20-25 minutes.

Transfer to an airtight container and freeze for at least 2 hours before serving.

Mojito Sorbet

Servings: 6-8

Ingredients

2 cups water

3/4 cup sugar

1 cup fresh lime juice

1/2 cup white rum

1/4 cup fresh mint leaves, finely chopped

Instructions

In a saucepan, heat water and sugar until sugar is dissolved. Let cool.

In a large bowl, combine cooled sugar syrup, lime juice, rum, and mint leaves. Stir well.

Chill the mixture in the refrigerator for at least 2 hours.

Pour the chilled mixture into the Cuisinart ice cream maker and churn for 20-25 minutes.

Transfer to an airtight container and freeze for at least 2 hours before serving.

Watermelon Vodka Sorbet

Servings: 6-8

Ingredients

4 cups watermelon, seeded and pureed

1/2 cup vodka

3/4 cup sugar

1/4 cup lime juice

Instructions

In a large bowl, combine watermelon puree, vodka, sugar, and lime juice. Stir until sugar is dissolved.

Chill the mixture in the refrigerator for at least 2 hours.

Pour the chilled mixture into the Cuisinart ice cream maker and churn for 20-25 minutes.

Transfer to an airtight container and freeze for at least 2 hours before serving.

Frozen Peach Bellini

Servings: 6-8

Ingredients

2 cups fresh peaches, peeled and pureed

1 cup Prosecco

1/2 cup sugar

1/4 cup lemon juice

Instructions

In a large bowl, combine peach puree, Prosecco, sugar, and lemon juice. Stir until sugar is dissolved.

Chill the mixture in the refrigerator for at least 2 hours.

Pour the chilled mixture into the Cuisinart ice cream maker and churn for 20-25 minutes.

Transfer to an airtight container and freeze for at least 2 hours before serving.

Frozen Irish Coffee

Servings: 6-8

Ingredients

2 cups strong brewed coffee, cooled

1 cup heavy cream

1/2 cup Irish whiskey

3/4 cup sugar

1 tablespoon vanilla extract

Instructions

In a large bowl, combine coffee, heavy cream, Irish whiskey, sugar, and vanilla extract. Stir until sugar is dissolved.

Chill the mixture in the refrigerator for at least 2 hours.

Pour the chilled mixture into the Cuisinart ice cream maker and churn for 25-30 minutes.

Transfer to an airtight container and freeze for at least 2 hours before serving.

Blackberry Gin Sorbet

Servings: 6-8

Ingredients

2 cups fresh blackberries, pureed

1 cup water

1/2 cup gin

3/4 cup sugar

1/4 cup lemon juice

Instructions

In a large bowl, combine blackberry puree, water, gin, sugar, and lemon juice. Stir until sugar is dissolved.

Chill the mixture in the refrigerator for at least 2 hours.

Pour the chilled mixture into the Cuisinart ice cream maker and churn for 20-25 minutes.

Transfer to an airtight container and freeze for at least 2 hours before serving.

Frozen Sangria

Servings: 6-8

Ingredients

2 cups red wine

1 cup orange juice

1/2 cup brandy

3/4 cup sugar

1 cup mixed berries (strawberries, blueberries, raspberries), pureed

Instructions

In a large bowl, combine red wine, orange juice, brandy, sugar, and berry puree. Stir until sugar is dissolved.

Chill the mixture in the refrigerator for at least 2 hours.

Pour the chilled mixture into the Cuisinart ice cream maker and churn for 20-25 minutes.

Transfer to an airtight container and freeze for at least 2 hours before serving.

Frozen Lemon Drop

Servings: 6-8

Ingredients

1 cup fresh lemon juice

1 cup water

1/2 cup vodka

3/4 cup sugar

1 tablespoon lemon zest

Instructions

In a large bowl, combine lemon juice, water, vodka, sugar, and lemon zest. Stir until sugar is dissolved.

Chill the mixture in the refrigerator for at least 2 hours.

Pour the chilled mixture into the Cuisinart ice cream maker and churn for 20-25 minutes.

Transfer to an airtight container and freeze for at least 2 hours before serving.

Mango Rum Sorbet

Servings: 6-8

Ingredients

2 cups fresh mango, pureed

1 cup water

1/2 cup rum

3/4 cup sugar

1/4 cup lime juice

Instructions

In a large bowl, combine mango puree, water, rum, sugar, and lime juice. Stir until sugar is dissolved.

Chill the mixture in the refrigerator for at least 2 hours.

Pour the chilled mixture into the Cuisinart ice cream maker and churn for 20-25 minutes.

Transfer to an airtight container and freeze for at least 2 hours before serving.

Frozen Cosmopolitan

Servings: 6-8

Ingredients

1 cup cranberry juice

1/2 cup vodka

1/4 cup triple sec

3/4 cup sugar

1/4 cup lime juice

Instructions

In a large bowl, combine cranberry juice, vodka, triple sec, sugar, and lime juice. Stir until sugar is dissolved.

Chill the mixture in the refrigerator for at least 2 hours. Pour the chilled mixture into the Cuisinart ice cream maker and churn for 20-25 minutes.

Transfer to an airtight container and freeze for at least 2 hours before serving.

Tropical Rum Sorbet

Servings: 6-8

Ingredients

1 cup pineapple juice

1 cup coconut milk

1/2 cup rum

3/4 cup sugar

1/4 cup orange juice

Instructions

In a large bowl, combine pineapple juice, coconut milk, rum, sugar, and orange juice. Stir until sugar is dissolved.

Chill the mixture in the refrigerator for at least 2 hours.

Pour the chilled mixture into the Cuisinart ice cream maker and churn for 20-25 minutes.

Transfer to an airtight container and freeze for at least 2 hours before serving.

Frozen Blueberry Mojito

Servings: 6-8

Ingredients

2 cups fresh blueberries, pureed

1 cup water

1/2 cup white rum

3/4 cup sugar

1/4 cup lime juice

1/4 cup fresh mint leaves, finely chopped

Instructions

In a large bowl, combine blueberry puree, water, rum, sugar, lime juice, and mint leaves. Stir until sugar is dissolved.

Chill the mixture in the refrigerator for at least 2 hours. Pour the chilled mixture into the Cuisinart ice cream maker and churn for 20-25 minutes.

Transfer to an airtight container and freeze for at least 2 hours before serving.

Frozen Pineapple Basil Margarita

Servings: 6-8

Ingredients

2 cups fresh pineapple, pureed

1 cup water

1/2 cup tequila

1/4 cup triple sec

3/4 cup sugar

1/4 cup lime juice

1/4 cup fresh basil leaves, finely chopped

Instructions

In a large bowl, combine pineapple puree, water, tequila, triple sec, sugar, lime juice, and basil leaves. Stir until sugar is dissolved.

Chill the mixture in the refrigerator for at least 2 hours.

Pour the chilled mixture into the Cuisinart ice cream maker and churn for 20-25 minutes.

Transfer to an airtight container and freeze for at least 2 hours before serving.

Frozen Cherry Bourbon

Servings: 6-8

Ingredients

2 cups fresh cherries, pitted and pureed

1 cup water

1/2 cup bourbon

3/4 cup sugar

1/4 cup lemon juice

Instructions

In a large bowl, combine cherry puree, water, bourbon, sugar, and lemon juice. Stir until sugar is dissolved.

Chill the mixture in the refrigerator for at least 2 hours.

Pour the chilled mixture into the Cuisinart ice cream maker and churn for 20-25 minutes.

Transfer to an airtight container and freeze for at least 2 hours before serving.

Frozen Raspberry Martini

Servings: 6-8

Ingredients

2 cups fresh raspberries, pureed

1 cup water

1/2 cup vodka

1/4 cup triple sec

3/4 cup sugar

1/4 cup lemon juice

Instructions

In a large bowl, combine raspberry puree, water, vodka, triple sec, sugar, and lemon juice. Stir until sugar is dissolved.

Chill the mixture in the refrigerator for at least 2 hours. Pour the chilled mixture into the Cuisinart ice cream maker and churn for 20-25 minutes.

Transfer to an airtight container and freeze for at least 2 hours before serving.

Frozen Cucumber Gin Fizz

Servings: 6-8

Ingredients

2 cups cucumber, peeled and pureed

1 cup water

1/2 cup gin

3/4 cup sugar

1/4 cup lime juice

1/4 cup fresh mint leaves, finely chopped

Instructions

In a large bowl, combine cucumber puree, water, gin, sugar, lime juice, and mint leaves. Stir until sugar is dissolved.

Chill the mixture in the refrigerator for at least 2 hours.

Pour the chilled mixture into the Cuisinart ice cream maker and churn for 20-25 minutes.

Transfer to an airtight container and freeze for at least 2 hours before serving.

Frozen Kiwi Mojito

Servings: 6-8

Ingredients

2 cups fresh kiwi, peeled and pureed

1 cup water

1/2 cup white rum

3/4 cup sugar

1/4 cup lime juice

1/4 cup fresh mint leaves, finely chopped

Instructions

In a large bowl, combine kiwi puree, water, rum, sugar, lime juice, and mint leaves. Stir until sugar is dissolved.

Chill the mixture in the refrigerator for at least 2 hours.

Pour the chilled mixture into the Cuisinart ice cream maker and churn for 20-25 minutes.

Transfer to an airtight container and freeze for at least 2 hours before serving.

Frozen Grapefruit Campari Sorbet

Servings: 6-8

Ingredients

2 cups fresh grapefruit juice

1 cup water

1/2 cup Campari

3/4 cup sugar

Instructions

In a large bowl, combine grapefruit juice, water, Campari, and sugar. Stir until sugar is dissolved.

Chill the mixture in the refrigerator for at least 2 hours.

Pour the chilled mixture into the Cuisinart ice cream maker and churn for 20-25 minutes.

Transfer to an airtight container and freeze for at least 2 hours before serving.

Frozen Lime Margarita

Servings: 6-8

Ingredients

1 cup fresh lime juice

1 cup water

1/2 cup tequila

1/4 cup triple sec

3/4 cup sugar

Instructions

In a large bowl, combine lime juice, water, tequila, triple sec, and sugar. Stir until sugar is dissolved.

Chill the mixture in the refrigerator for at least 2 hours. Pour the chilled mixture into the Cuisinart ice cream maker and churn for 20-25 minutes.

Transfer to an airtight container and freeze for at least 2 hours before serving.

Frozen Pineapple Rum Sorbet

Servings: 6-8

Ingredients

2 cups fresh pineapple, pureed

1 cup water

1/2 cup rum

3/4 cup sugar

1/4 cup lime juice

Instructions

In a large bowl, combine pineapple puree, water, rum, sugar, and lime juice. Stir until sugar is dissolved.

Chill the mixture in the refrigerator for at least 2 hours.

Pour the chilled mixture into the Cuisinart ice cream maker and churn for 20-25 minutes.

Transfer to an airtight container and freeze for at least 2 hours before serving.

Frozen Banana Daiquiri

Servings: 6-8

Ingredients

2 ripe bananas, mashed

1 cup water

1/2 cup rum

3/4 cup sugar

1/4 cup lime juice

Instructions

In a large bowl, combine mashed bananas, water, rum, sugar, and lime juice. Stir until sugar is dissolved. Chill the mixture in the refrigerator for at least 2 hours.

Pour the chilled mixture into the Cuisinart ice cream maker and churn for 20-25 minutes.

Transfer to an airtight container and freeze for at least 2 hours before serving.

Recipe Index

About the Author

Sarah Aubert is passionate about empowering people to lead active healthy lifestyles by teaching them the personalized skills they need to fuel themselves with whole foods while maintaining a healthy life balance.

Made in United States
Troutdale, OR
12/20/2024

26993777R00058